Twin Flames

Abigail Byrne

BookLeaf Publishing

Twin Flames © 2022 Abigail Byrne

All rights reserved.

No part of this publication may be reproduced, stored in a retrieval system, or transmitted, in any form or by any means, electronic, mechanical, photocopying, recording or otherwise, without the prior written permission of the presenters.

Abigail Byrne asserts the moral right to be identified as author of this work.

Presentation by *BookLeaf Publishing*

Web: www.bookleafpub.com

E-mail: info@bookleafpub.com

ISBN: 9789395255189

First edition 2022

DEDICATION

My love of poetry began with reading Funky
Chickens by Benjamin Zephaniah in year one,
to him for making me realise early on that
words can dance and jump.

Ashley Lister, Charlie Hart and Colin Davies,
mega authors who always take the time to read
my little ditties that I do nothing with.

Mr McCabe. The scariest high school English
teacher to have lived, he always made time to
read my teen angst poetry and encourage my
passion. As well, Mr Karoonian for teaching me
that being me is just fine.

And to Shane Koyczan, it's not often you get to
meet your hero and it be an amazing
experience. I told him I wanted to publish a
book one day and he said "do it" so I am.

Most importantly, to my cat, Haggis. He can't
read though so I needn't say any more.

ACKNOWLEDGEMENT

Joanna Anyon has been my friend since we were know it all teenagers in school. I thank her for knowing me well enough and putting up with me long enough to make me aware of this opportunity.

To my dad for listening to every poem I've written since I was six and being my biggest (and possibly only) fan.

To my mum for not committing infanticide.

To Charlie McCarthey, for being my twin flame, for building me up brick by brick, cell by cell.

Rem, thank you for being who you are.

To my poor husband who puts up with me squealing with joy when I see ducks.

PREFACE

I googled "book preface" - it means the reason a book was written, apparently. This book came to be, here in your hands, to be read. The contents however came about through my experiences and observations, stuff that tickled me or made me mardy.

Kirsty's Hymn

The earth is the church,
The trees, they are the steeple,
The clouds are all scriptures,
Free to all the world's people.
The rivers recite the psalms,
The birds sing songs of praise,
High peaks expand with gratefulness,
Each soul to the sky does raise.
The seas are true disciples,
The wind and the rain are the word,
No building can contain the gods,
For the godly is the world.
I see the holy in beauty,
The divinity of truth,
In every outline of your golden worth,
I see it pouring out of you.
Landscapes change with time,
Flowers blossom and trees fall,
But there's a certain grace that's gifted,
To a leaning tree that won't fall.
So plant your routes down deeper,
You're someone's favourite place to sit,
Come wind or rain or hail,
But darling, do not quit.

The Silver Vixen

When I'm an old lady,
I'll make friends with crows,
I'll talk to trees,
I'll re-pierce my nose.
When I'm an old lady,
I'll steal tea spoons,
I'll wear band tees and leggings,
And howl at the moon.
When I'm an old lady,
I'll still be tattooed and weird;
With the kind of house that looks haunted and
feared.
I'll age disgracefully,
I'll laugh distastefully,
Like a witch,
With garish ambition.
I'll plant wild flowers,
Sing in public showers,
I'll be a nuisance,
Of that I am sure.
My wild ways I won't quit,
I'll be quite the shit,
When I'm an old lady,
And I'll settle the score.

19th November, Every Year

The kinda gal who doesn't wear make up,
The kinda gal who piles it on,
Both of these gals have their reasons,
Neither of them are wrong.
The kinda gal who is cis,
The kinda gal who ain't,
The kinda gal who's into gaming,
The kinda gal who prefers to paint.
The kinda gal who likes to party,
The kinda gal who don't,
The kinda gal who'll shag on a first date,
And the kinda gal who won't.
The kinda gal who gets on with the lads,
The kinda gal who likes brunch with the girls,
The kinda gal who's career is life,
The kinda gal who's kids are her world.
The kinda gals who write poems,
Tattoos or rides motorbikes,
Our medics, coppers,
Stiletto flip-floppers,
On international women's day.

Cliche

4

We'll burn that bridge when we get to it,
It isn't that we can't go back,
It to stop dead wood from cracking beneath us,
It's a quite deliberate act.
It's to stop the unwanted following us,
To prevent a boundary from being crossed,
A metaphor for screaming out:
Fuck off, good night, get lost!

Spot the Difference

5

For every refugee.

We kiss our babies goodnight,
She may be kissing hers goodbye.
We groan when our babies cry,
She rejoices: hers didn't die.

We take our babies to family,
Her family didn't make it.
We hush at the neighbour's noise,
She hopes the bombings don't wake it.

We smile as they take their first steps,
Their first steps could be their last.
We shelter our babies from scary sights,
She shelters hers from the blasts.

We lay our babies down to sleep,
In a little Moses basket,
She lays her baby down to sleep,
In a little, tiny casket.

Fossil Fuel Sin

We don't move like there's a motion,
We don't breathe like we've a goal,
We don't touch because we're supposed to,
We burn like we're coal.
Like we've been under pressure for millennia,
Forming buried deep,
Spat out by the earth,
Waking from our sleep.
We could have turned to diamonds,
But we emerge to burn,
Him and me we're fire,
Creating ashes to fill the urn.
We throw at each other our skeletons;
Our closets laid bare,
Our skin on skin,
Our fossil fuel sin;
He's my favourite thing to wear.
We fuck like corporate giants,
We make love like the moonlight kisses the sea,
Where he's the ocean I'm a paper boat,
He's going to capsize me.
He's the one to come up for breath,
I will sink all the way down,
To the bottom of the world with him,
Where I will gladly drown.

Pass Me a Rubber

If poetry could make you smile,
I'd write a few lines for you,
If poetry could cure all ills,
Then write is all that I'd do.
If poetry was a super power,
I'd write to save the day,
If poetry was an STD,
Then I'd be bangin away.
If poetry was an std,
Then I would fuck the world,
Rhyming my way through the population,
Of every consenting (appropriately aged)
Guy and girl.
If poetry was an std,
I'd let my juices flow,
I'd form a rhyming couplet,
Wherever I could go.
I'd be onomatopoeia on you,
Slapping the lines into your soul,
I'd be tearing you down and filling you up,
Poetry in every hole.
If poetry was an std,
Then I would be a whore,
But poetry ain't an std,
So bumpin uglies is a chore.

Instead I'll just sit at home,
Where my poetry packs it's own clout,
I shall instead refer to writing,
As the art of rubbing one out.

Pray For Rain

Stick me on a pyre,
Stack the logs up high,
Load it up with petrol,
Flick the match to hear me cry.
But there's a little something you don't see,
Something you didn't quite learn,
I'm a fire walker darling,
And I refuse to burn.
Take heed of the embers,
Feel the ash rain as it falls,
Watch my mighty dancing shadow,
I'm little, way up tall.

I'm a fire Walker baby,
There's pain in my soles and in my soul,
I'll take the heat,
Ten thousand feet,
I refuse to fall.
So throw at me every canister,
Lit furious firework,
I'm a fire Walker, bastard,
You'll not send me berserk.

Oh my darling, oh my love,
Oh sweet jesus in the heavens above,

I know my way around fire,
Like a lit fuse,
Tick tick boom,
You will wilt before I burn out,
I'll consume the entire room.
I'm fuelling my own fire,
Feel the heat of my molotov heart,
Ashen, ablaze and devastated,
These flames will never part.

I'm a fire walker,
Sweetheart,
I'm just doing what I do.
I'll walk the coals like they're beaten streets,
And I'll walk away from you.

Windmills

I'm the ripples of a pebble,
That someone threw into a lake,
I'm the stubborn line remaining;
The non erased mistake.
I'm the footprint in the sand,
Washed in part by sea,
I'm the fourth person there,
When the invite stated three.
I'm the other end of the phone call,
Answered in a pocket,
I'm the discarded photo,
From a second hand locket.
I'm a moment in a moment,
One you'll soon forget,
I'm a decision taken lightly,
That's easy to regret.
I'm a wheel within a wheel,
A cog you can replace,
Just know that I love you all,
I'm not one to forget a face.

Crude Kittens

I love my hairless pussy,
Sleek and smooth and fine,
There are many hairless pussies,
My favourite one is mine.
I love to stroke the soft skin,
All night and all day,
My hairless Pussy has a mind of its own,
And sometimes wants a play.
I bet your thinking this is a bit saucy,
That I'm really a bit of a minx,
My hairless pussy is a cat,
A lovely little sphynx!

Meet me at The Moon

I'm off to sleep, I lie.
I lie and stare,
Wide awake wondering what it'll take to turn
off.
Because when your body's full of adrenaline,
You're jittering not mellowing,
And your nerves are on fire,
It sounds great,
But it's now quarter to 8am and you went to bed
at 11.
You get up,
On a winter's morn,
You greet the sun and mourn the moon,
She offers a chance at rest.
But unlike the rest,
You don't.
They say sunrise is a romantic thing to witness,
Then call my pain-induced insomnia an act of
self love,
Where my nerves set on end,
And my only friend,
Is the quiet creaking, sneaking of the floorboards
beneath my feet,
As I measure defeat,
And pop the kettle on.

At night,
I see hedgehogs and bed hogs,
The slug from the sink.
The old toad in the garden,
When I sit for a drink.
I see blue lights,
And new lights,
New days come to greet,
I see the moon kissed by the sun,
Just swept off her feet.
I'm off to sleep, I lie.

Be Still

15

If statues could move,
Every mother Madonna would hang her head in
shame.
Every cherub,
Would lay down their bow and still their wings
at the mention of your name.
The angels would turn away,
Their pious faces now a grimace.
Lincoln would resign from his seat,
The chiseled doves,
Their wings would beat a furious hum of
indignation.
At the state of your nation,
Lady Liberty would throw down her torch,
And shout in fury:
I stand for you no more.

Plutonic

I say old soul,
As I've met them before.
We've walked the same path,
We've opened each door.
Not years ago,
But waves ago timeless,
And here we are,
Meeting again,
Priceless.
And if all we are,
Are particles and dust,
Let our bones fuse together,
Let our iron blood rust.
If we are but illusion,
Let us be the lights in the sky,
Dancing through clouds,
Drawing each curious eye.
And if we be real,
Set in this repose,
Let the universe sing,
A song everyone knows.
And if hope is hopeless,
I want those I was gifted to see,
That I'm thankful for the universe,
For sending them to me.

Disabling Language

When you're talkin about nasty words,
It can really be a farce,
If I want to make bottom "dirty",
I'd switch the word for arse.
There's many words for penis,
Yer cock, your knob, ones dick,
There's a multitude of phallic phrases,
One needs to take one's pick,
We can talk about the fanny,
The twat, the clunge, the minge,
Or we can go a sinister route and REALLY
make you cringe.
I could say a word,
That I really know I shun't,
But calling someone "differently abled",
Makes you a bit of a cunt.
I can sit here and say fuckers,
Wankers, dickhead, twat.
But the word disabled makes folks
uncomfortable,
Who'd have thought of that?

No One's Come For Tea

No one was a friend of hers,
No one looked at her with a kind eye,
No one played with her at lunch,
Some days no one made her cry.
No one sang along with her,
No one held her hand,
No one read stories with her,
No one played with her in the sand.
No one pushed the boys down the stairs,
No one pulled out the girls hair,
No one stood beside her,
No one, stood right there.
"I think they will be kinder now"
She whispered when she was done,
Her mother screamed when she found the body.
"It wasn't me, it was no one!"!

Odds Against The Favourite

So it's off to the races today?
Glad rags on,
A little flutter, you say?
The bookies lines as long as they can get,
An adrenaline filled day,
On that you can bet!
Into the starting gate they go,
Will they all make it?
Well we just don't know.
The big grand beasts,
They glisten with sweat,
They ran really hard,
You bet!

And broken winded,
Ulcered stomachs they walk,
The punters cheer,
The trainers talk,
And I sit here,
Quite upset,
Because five of them died,
Because;
YOU BET.

You played a part,
Yes you,
For fun.
Don't argue with me,
"But they love to run"
The part that you don't seem to get,
Is they don't love to suffer,
You bet!

I bet they hurt,
I bet their lives are short,
I bet they're old age,
Is an afterthought.
I bet you can name a few of the greats,
I bet there's no profit,
In their fallen mates.

So call me spoil sport,
Question me why,
My answer is this;
You bet,
They die.

Empathy

Put out all the stars,
And take away the light,
Banish all that's beautiful,
As I have no use for sight.

Steal the notes from the music,
Steal the sweet song from each bird,
As I begged and cried please leave me be,
Yet he did not hear a word.

Take the sunrise from the sun
The deep blue from the sea,
Take away all that is magical,
As I had that taken from me.

Dull the sweetness in the sugar,
Dull the zing out of each spice,
Wipe the smiles off of every child,
Why should anyone experience what's nice?

He had the passion in my heart,
He had the hope within my mind,
He's more than welcome to all the rest,
As I've been left so blind.

Too Bendy to Break

You can rip at my arms,
They'll come out of their sockets,
But I remain together.
You can weigh me down with bandages,
And braces,
I'll remain as light as a feather.

You can bend me backwards,
Until my vertebrae move,
But believe me,
I will not break.
You can force me down,
Right in the crowd,
You can do what you think it will take.

You can hide in me,
Dormant for months,
In my DNA you remain concealed,
You can push me and pull me,
Hush me, control me,
But to you,
I will never yield.

Mr. McNairy's Magical Act!

Mr. McNairy's magical act,
Will leave you astounded,
That is a fact,
With his ladies and saws,
And boxes and more,
And rabbits in hats,
That the whole crowd will adore!

Just one night,
The show about to start,
His little bunny,
Had a change of heart.
'You grab at my ears,
After stuffing me in a hat!
Well I say no more,
And that is that!'

'Nonsense!' Yelled McNairy,
Going red in the face,
'You're my main feature,
The show would be a disgrace!'

He grabbed Bunny's ears,
And crammed him in tight,
Little bunny played dumb,

Little bunny didn't fight.

At the end of the show,
McNairy went to bed,
The pound signs and applause,
Running about in his head.
He closed his eyes,
Whilst he was sleeping,
He didn't hear the sounds,
Of poor bunny weeping.

'He pulls my ears,
It hurts you know!
I think it's high time,
That I had a go!'

Bunny got the hat,
And hopped to the bed,
Where Mr. McNairy,
Was resting his head.
He tied the ties,
And got out the saw,
McNairy screamed,
Until his throat was raw.

'You were too big,
To fit in the hat,
A few alterations,
Corrected that!'
Said bunny,
As he grabbed old McNairy's hair,
He dragged him,
And placed him,
Just,
Over,
There.
'For the final encore,
Our very last act!
Watch a bunny,
Pull a magician,
Right out from a hat!'

And bunny yanked,
On McNairy's old ears,
With a manic laugh,
And happy tears,
'Behold' he said,
'The great McNairy,
And his faithful sidekick,
Fluffy McScary!'

You Lost...

The tide is changing,
Howling gales declare,
Every shoreline, everywhere,
Go breach your banks,
Attack the land with sodden tanks;
Make humanity kneel,
Every shoreline, everywhere,

Must lose.

Dust

I wish my skin would crawl away,
Flee from every bone,
It can rest somewhere in sanctuary,
And leave me here alone.
Maybe I'll be comfortable,
Without that clinging skin,
Maybe I'd see something worthy,
Find some beauty within.
Or maybe I'd just bleed to death,
Shedding who I am,
Maybe my mind is playing tricks,
Maybe it's all a scam.
Maybe I will never know,
But I'll try my best,
I must,
As today I am flesh and bone,
And one day I'll be dust.

www.ingramcontent.com/pod-product-compliance
Lightning Source LLC
LaVergne TN
LVHW021335200726
843509LV00014B/2541